VIA Folios 166

What? Nothing

Dialogs on Sovereign Decreation

What?
Nothing

Dialogs on Sovereign Decreation

Willi Q Minn

BORDIGHERA PRESS

for
The wagoning poet of 125 South John St.

Library of Congress Control Number: 2023952373

Published by
BORDIGHERA PRESS
John D. Calandra Italian American Institute
25 W. 43rd Street, 17th Floor
New York, NY 10036

VIA Folios 166
ISBN 978-1-59954-213-3

Table of Contents

Preface

These poems traffic in the day to day living of two talking heads, Giulia and Willi – residents in the barrier island Lido di Venezia, wizened by forty years of transatlantic crossings between Italy and the United States and now made idle by age and their forced removal from the public sphere of work. Clinging like exhausted swimmers to the forgotten creeds of western democracy, wherein every person is purportedly king and queen unto themselves, they take their dubious status to heart by wielding their metaphors with mortal irony.

It's not our youth that we are losing; it's our old age; and old age is worthless in our time. (an observation by W. E. B. Du Bois, *The Autobiography*)

"There is a sliver of my American imagination that wavers at the thought of self and ego falling away, the individual in our culture having been endowed with godlike sanctity, or so it would seem." (Tracy K. Smith, *To Free the Captives*)

An Aside

These domestic commotions may seem as errant as a remark by
Lydia Davis, a sigh from Samuel Beckett, or the 'I do this, I do
that' chatter of Frank O'Hara; but they have a topical focus all
their own, are consciously diasporic and anchored in different
geographies. Some of the poems are last-minute dispatches, others
knifelike snippets of offhand conversation instigated by a passing
remark and riposte. 'Texticules,' Beckett would have called some
of them. If given quarter, they may offer glimpses into the prodigal
and citric intimacy emerging from the oral exchanges of two heads
who have lived long lives side by side and are now suiting up
for the endgame with wide-open, almost sightless eyes. Without
having to say so, they have vowed to each other, "We haven't come
this far only to come this far." Readers with the ocean in their ears
will understand.

DRAMATIS PERSONAE

A word about Giulia:

"Ella sorrise alquanto, e poi 'S'elli erra
L'opinion', mi disse, 'de' mortali,
dove chiave di senso non diserra,
    certo non ti dovrien punger li strali
d'ammirazione omai, poi dietro ai sensi
vedi che la ragione ha corte l'ali'."
(Dante, *Paradiso* 2.52-57)

"She smiled a little, and then said to me,
'If the opinion of men errs in matters
which the key of our senses cannot unlock,
surely wonder's arrows should not pierce you
from this point on, since even when you follow
the senses, you see that reason's wings fall short.'"

A quote from Willi: "Et ideo dico quod iudicium medium est apprehensionis et appetitus; nam primo res apprehenditur, deinde apprehensa bona vel mala iudicatur, et ultimo iudicans prosequitur sive fugit. [. . .] si vero ab appetitu quocunque modo proveniente iudicium moveatur, liberum esse non potest, quia non a se, sed ab alio captivum trahitur." (Dante, *Monarchia* I.12.3-4)

"Judgment, therefore, I declare, is the link between perception and appetite, for first of all a thing is perceived, then it is judged to be good or bad, and finally the one doing the judging either pursues or rejects it. [. . .] but if judgment is at all preempted and thus controlled by desire, it cannot be free, for it does not now act of its own accord, but is dragged along captive to another."
(Dante, *On World Government*, trans. Herbert Schneider)

Endgame

Endgame

Willi, are you awake?
I brought you some chocolate cake.

I'll take it with me.

Can you talk?

Can you hear me?

This morning I was thinking
about your endgame stand
on sovereign being. Can we
return to it one more time?

I'm done with my books.
They've taken my cane.

So in the end sovereignty
and being human are about
embodiment, huh?

In the end, it's about bare life,
like me here in this bed,
without pajamas.

the barely human . . .

               the fully human.

"*Ecce Homo!*" Behold
the woman, Pilate said.

Behold King Lear, Act V,
Willi sighs instead.

So it's sovereignty
by way of reduction
and subtraction?
You with all those
tubes and needles,
me with just my pension
and bad knees?

It's essence as existence,
one person at a time,
the Lido our reign
where we lay our
burden down.

But without Incarnation? Or
the Second Coming? Just food
a shoeshine and shelter?
Jack and Jill went up the hill?

No books no cane.
It's me, you, what's left.
Coursing through this pain
I hear the shoring waters
of Winnebago lapping . . .
May your prayers
send me back.

So that's it, that's
our sovereign being?
Living each wave,
then up the flue?

Me and you. Just
us two.

Well, try to get
some rest today.
And try not to talk
so much it tires you.

Every day is Sunday here,
like in Via Lepanto
since we retired
thirty years ago.

Oh Lordy.

Dear Moon, July 2019

Pressing Giulia
Willi snorts,

Do you care
for me at all,
at all?

Sometimes
I love you
always,
Giulia clarifies
through the half-
closed door of
her den.

Leaning Inward

Leaning inward
we hold each other up,
coffee pills and wine
in the same cracked cup.

In the morning bright Marì
scats her family's news;
when she's gone,
we repeat it like a blues.

The days go fast,
the days go slow,
we relive the past,
in shades of woe.

Spheres of Influence

Somebody put
the refrigerator shelves
in backwards.

*Well, Willi, why
don't you fix it?*

Anybody
can see they're
in wrong.

Giulia, Reading Virgil in Bed

Here we go!
She says fairly falling
falling off
to slee
      eee
         p

Willi to his Muse

(Harrowed, bent-over, fallow)

I come to you chastened
a suppliant, forgive me
this eleventh hour flirt,
as if we hadn't already
met at Dr. Scaramuccia's
that time he failed to show
oh how many moons ago.

A Kingdom of Prospects

With one grand gesture
she flipped
the folded comforter
over the tumulus
of his stomach
to his crowning
satisfaction

Growing Farther and Farther Together

Pippin?

What?

Did you make some coffee?

Yup.

*I thought I
smelled something
in the air.*

Yup, there's still
something there.

Not Everything Can Be Explained

You know I like
your guest, for guests
are holy even here
in via Lepanto,
as long as they
don't clinger.

You telling me?
Santissimo mio,
we can always
add water
to the beans.

Three stars, Giulia!
That way they won't stick.

Giulia the '68er

I guess the mayor was right after all.
This stone-paved plaza sure is popular:
parents, skateboarders, that pooping dog.

I still remember the beautiful park
buried underneath it, and the cool shade
trees in place of the bleached white stone.

Either the park or the plaza, remember it was
an election year about progress and change.
Us greenies? We couldn't fill a Volkswagen.

Ah, Willi, I still hear the cicadas stirring.
Can you hear them? They're all around.

You're making it up. I can't hear a thing.

You kidding? Why, they're deafening!

Ceremony

You gotta be
kidding:

there he is
again,

old papa Teo
Arrivabene,

bereft of wife a
year ago,

stalled again at
high noon

on his rusty three-wheel
bicycle

at the bottom of
the rise

of via Bragadin
bridge

over Lepanto
canal

sitting perfectly
still

waiting for the school
children

to come along
and

surprise him
with

a push from
behind.

Backyard Cosmology

Willi, will you put
the statue of the virgin
on top of that stone?
It makes a perfect fit.
It makes the stone a globe.
She graces the grass.

A stone is a stone is
a stone, can't you see?
His male glare breaking
against the neighbor's
fortlike backyard wall.

She betrays her
fright to him, fearing
for a moment he might
be speaking a fiery
bipartisan truth. But
only for a flickering:

There! That makes
a world of difference,
at least for the yard,
she thrills.

The statue reigns
on the globe, embracing
Willi and the neighbor
in an original relation of
grace and grass and stone —
ora che ci penso.

The Two Bodies of the Queen

("If at night. . . like a broken king")

On the night of
his 76th birthday
in deepest gloom,
a touching moment
with the queen:

In falling asleep
she happens
to slip her
big toe
snuggly up
against his
royal anus.

Taken aback,
stirred to the root,
he dared
not move:

Simply put,
I did not want
to disturb her
majesty.

Sovereignty, What?

You know, Willi, now
that we are fare-thee-well
royalty what does that
demotion mean?
Kings and queens sit idle
on their thrones and enjoy
a gawking entourage.
Since we've retired it's
as if we disappeared,
mouth stopped up and
grass to the world. Who
are we to be listening?

You think growing old is
some kind of failure? As if
we were benumbed by the past
unfolding before us? Memory's
crusaders, mikes for its memes?
Take comfort, cara, *in being*
retired, carefree and fully
at rest, we're as near to being
human as newborn babes.
Eye on the dailies at Bar
Fortuna in the square; for
the price of a double espresso
you can pose for the tourists,
the island's regina del giorno.

"Live as if the world?" *Glaub Treu*!
No jumping, shouting or dancing?
No stripping, coupling or Lido juju?
From pink dawn to sunset blinding!

Our rights, Giulia! 1789. All
careers and crafts end equally
in rest. Twittering? If it doesn't pay
it must be idle play. Lafargue!

Like flopping in a chair and napping
while Marì mops the floor?
That eternal master/slave rapport!
Remember Schmitt: It's making
decisions and having the power
to command. Or what's a queen for?

Sovereignty, Giulia, is only
a way of naming your spectral
humanity. You dear queer were
despotic from day one, now
the Lido's storied pittima.

Good luck in dividing my
inborn pluck from my
abstract royalty. *Das Kapital!*
You truly believe you can pry me
apart in layers? How easy it is
to become a Lido nobody.

We're talking philosophy, Giulia,
our fight for rights even when senile,
not personal anecdote or your lack
of popularity in via Lepanto.

So, is sovereignty the same worldwide?
The same for the Uyghurs in China?
The same for the Standing Rock Sioux?
The same for you, my necktop alien?

Let's stick closer to home for
a change, Okay? Stop buzzing around
like Emily's bee — sting and wing —
to keep me at bay.

And you? You sound like a talking head.
Let's knock it off till tomorrow.
It's time to go to bed.

Sovereignty, Nothing

Willi, I think the rich can lord it over
the poor and enjoy a fuller life, don't you?
Success, fame, caviar: life is surely more
than us two vying to stay alive, huh?

Ah, but the rich and the poor are equally
sovereign, or we'd end up with a world
boosting the rich and the spenders,
not us poor pensioners. Respect is not
about how many shoes you can hoard
or whether I drive a Porsche or a Ford.

I see why philosophers will never make
the best sovereigns. Reason will never
outfox fake news let alone Lido ardor.
Head and heat, Willi-nilly, tango together.

And the scandal of the cross? the first
shall be last and the last first, Eschaton!
The rapper to the cop, "It ain't no fun
when the rabbit got the gun."

               But we're not wagging
about Judgment Day, we're in via Lepanto
waiting for night to come, the game be done.
Bet there's a bit of *jihad* in both. At 41 kilos
I'll run with the rabbit and go with the gun.

At 41 kilos better hang with the cross;
time to confess your foibles and loss.

No time for jibes, my mirror, the chariot!
How long have you ignored my wailing?

Willi, Willi, when will you abandon me?

Hear hear, Giulia! We know I owe you me.
We're born indebted; who on earth can return
what's owed? A lifetime paying a boundless
ransom, then what?

It's the *what* that pesters me, and you.
Who will requite us, who embellish?

Well, why not offer your time for once,
help change our Lido street names:
a queen serving her neighborhood, honor
through errands. Sentiment de l'existence
or kenosis, *choose one or the other.*

Always foisting concepts on our referents!
My royalty is rooted here in via Lepanto;
yours? the whole blue planet's biosphere.
Sovereignty, you say, is a claim and a cause;
for me it's life this moment with all our flaws.

So, Giulia, deeds! Bring a bag of groceries
to bedridden Gianna; talk on the phone to Nori,
alone in Rome at ninety. The phone, Giulia!
They want to talk to you. Hurry or they will
charge the door, your ragtag retinue.

You know, Willi, in line at the Gate
it won't matter what you've read or
how well you quip, but whether
you answered the telephone. Your
hokey sovereignty!

What gate?

Cousin Nori, Where Are We Now?

Just now on the phone from Nori's
in Rome Giulia breaks me the news,
they diagnosed it as soft brain against
her will she'll have to be sent away
to a *casa di riposo* because she forgot
to turn off the gas on the kitchen stove
put the *prosciutto crudo* in with the
tablecloth left the water running in
the bidet (or was it the kitchen) had
all the lights on at noon and declined
to open the door to her neighbor a medic
who looked in on her none too soon.

Yesterday when I left the keys in the door
Giulia said Pay attention to what you're
doing OKAY? Last week I told her a story
about Einstein and his umbrella in Prague
and she said How many times you gonna
tell me that She didn't exactly call me
foggy but maybe thinking of cousin Nori
she huffed Willi Willi where's your head
they'll ship you to a home, you *here*?

I think I might already have told her
about oh What's-His-Name's radiant quip
the question's not Who am I but where
am I? Of course he's not from here; and
neither am I. I think I'll tell her anyway.

Giulia's Mountain Poetics

(Valcomelico Superiore, 18 May 2019)

Up Colisei trail Giulia hums almost gracefully,
far from Willi's petty intrigues. She sketches
an inner melody to accompany her resolute pace
going up, a laborious two-hour hike in harmony
with the small animals snoozing in their dens,
moles and mice in the underbrush thick with flare
of mushroom caps, myriad mosses, patches
of heather, holly, tall grasses and clutching vines.
The trail winds up and away among the dense firs
and beeches, larches and birches, spruces and pines,
all reaching upward like her; seedlings competing
for the sun's favors but rooted deep in the trickling
earth marked by years of rotting stumps, chainsaw
lumber jacks and logging logic, green on green, teeming
psychedelic theater of berry-stippled charm, dim
underworld receding step by step as Giulia climbs
above the treeline, determined to stand above
the world, above Friedrich the Wanderer and Willi,
level with the sky:

Stick to my pace, the path will lead me, my pace
and the path have a life of their own, far from Willi
and the valley below, its coffined fathering earth.

Giulia's Winter Mythology

(Valcomelico Superiore, 1 November 2018)

All the way down Colesei trail
stepping a galliard down to Lunelli,
your off-pitch melody scattering
upwards among the wing-harboring
firs, unfurling past fans of fern, oak leaf
downdraft, swaying of the resonant pines,
the choiring October forest swinging you
along soundways through wind-tuned scales,
you sing your native sunny tune, notes slipping
here and there among the loosened stones
and foot-snagging roots down the darkening
perilous path, a snaking two-hour descent down
to Lunelli Refuge for a season-ending feast
of polenta and porcini, cheese melt too,
and robust red wine: enough to make you
skid your way down Colesei trail, the arms
of your slicker green-vined loosely around
your hips to charm dull winter away for
yet another day, as if autumn's lingering
juju depended on you dispersing your tune
down Colesei trail, down to the valley below,
where sceptered Earth turns inward and silent
and the rioting hills yield to winter whiteout.

Squawk, A Genealogy

Forced by shipwreck to land
on Devil's Island, Somner's sailors
fed themselves on sea mews
so friendly and plentiful, they
decided to stay instead of starve
in gentleman-gloved Jamestown.

Our men found a pretty way to take them, which was by standing on
the rocks or sands by the seaside, and holloing, laughing, and making
the strangest outcry that possibly they could, with the noise whereof
the birds would come flocking to that place, and settle upon the very
arms and head of him that so cried, and still creep nearer and nearer,
answering the noise themselves; by which our men would weigh them
with their hand, and which weighed heaviest they took for the best and
let the others alone; and so our men would take twenty dozen in two
hours of the chiefest of them; and they were a good and well relished
fowl, fat and full as a partridge. (. . .) There are thousands of these
birds, and two or three islands full of their burrows (. . .) which birds,
for their blindness and for their cry and hooting, we called the "sea
owl." They will bite cruelly with their crooked bills.

* * *

Crossing Brooklyn ferry, he marked the sea-gulls,
caught them "high in the air floating with motionless
wings, oscillating their bodies . . . Fly on, sea-birds!
fly sideways, or wheel in large circles," stirring
Mannahatta's Ishmael to sail the seven seas.

"For the [city's] symbol, some collective presence
of great circling and plunging, hovering and
perching sea-birds, white-winged images of
the spirit, of the restless freedom of the Bay."

"How many dawns, chill from his rippling rest
The seagull's wings shall dip and pivot him,
Shedding white rings of tumult, building high
Over the chained bay waters Liberty—
Then, with inviolate curve, forsake our eyes."

*   *   *

In winter weather along our city's barrier island
the gulls vent themselves over morning mussels,
in a congress of squawking, capture and chase:
you strut these Lido beaches, big-bodied, keen,
wing-ranked, with Swiss-knife beak, down
these narrow shores to the San Nicolò breach.

Then late in May you work the tourist trade
like thugs in Saint Mark's Square, where
human swarms now flood the island suk;
from the Lido's Adriatic shores you crowd
the roof around the square in lapping cries,
dive for hors-d'oeuvres above Florian's
in a hurtling downdraft of burglars' wings,
rip crusts and cocktail rinds from trashbins
while lithe waiters dip and reel like *zanni*
with bowties, flying trays and scat of napkins.

Today the gulls of Strachey, Whitman, James
and Crane are gone; gulls for poets once were
signs: they soared and circled above our shores
invoking prayers, dreams, our barking souls.

In the bay the daily cruiseships blast away
leaving fish, fowl and UNESCO in dismay;
above the water's rising tide we all know
the Lido's gulls will hover, float and thrive
long after the summer tribes have gone away.

Now the Adriatic's Al Aaraaf and its hive
of humans serenely silent under the sea
are gone for good, while gusts of seagulls
dive for capitalist merchants' pearly skulls.

Wild Weather

The hard wind
hit the terrace,
then the rain hit:
the liquid wind
the wooshing rain.

Quick, shut the doors!

*Are the windows open
on the stairs?*

Oddio!

The wind and the rain
rock the building,
dance the two chairs,
and the ginkgo bends
like a messenger
in its pot.

Summertime, Climate Change I

(Willi ghostwrites a poem for Giulia)

The sun rises and stares, the heat invades
and occupies via Lepanto's sweaty flats;
the humidity polishes and clings from
Sunday to Sunday, morning, noon and
everywhere, through the brazen shuffle of
summer. From June through mid-September
Willi drags his shopping bag and can of Red
Bull to and fro along the fetid canal, hapless,
witless . . . waiting for the world to end.

Summertime, Climate Change II

(Giulia ghostwrites a poem for Willi)

The heat arrived undocumented from the South,
clandestine, by boat, without a college degree,
while a Saharan wind blew crafty knuckle balls
at elders in the square, knocking Giulia down.
The Morning Show's astrologist fiercely studied
the tattoos of his second for a sign, then mooned his
butt on air, after reporting a day of rain would end
the two-month drought exhaling in the riverbeds
of Veneto where seven boatmen played frisbee
from bank to bank, now that their savings were
gone with the wind and a random bolt from a UFO
beaned the fleeing prophet, laying him to rest.

Festa del Redentore

(17 July 2023)

*Google news bulletin: vast fire storms
afflict France, Portugal, and Spain
today, while England prepares for a
record heatwave.*

Thousands of boats in St Mark's bay tonight, the day's
headlines cry (Don't forget your reservation!). Tourists
from around the world, except for Russians, crush in,
attracted by a fix of consolation and fire flowers blessed
by our certified comic duo the cardinal and the mayor,
ready to sell the city to the lowest bidder: the kebab
and trinket shops, "pizza by the slice" and pasta ready
to go, where once there stood a *latteria* or *calzolaio*.

So let's go! Fireworks at midnight like you've never seen
before (not even in Vancouver) right behind the church
of the Redeemer, where cruising missiles brighten the sky
like those the Russians are firing night and day over Kyiv,
shooting stars aplenty and explosions with mushroom
tracers, and blood-red bursts of blinding light right out of
the fourth gospel. Distinctly a night of triumph for the lower
atmosphere: ghostly faces tilted upward, trancelike, to the super-
natural hijinxed sky, jubilant, tense, straining for something
to happen, billed as a call for peace: Boom! WHACWHAC
ᴢᴢZZZINGG! ʀʀRR-BOOOMMM! ZACPAM PUMPUM!

*Behind the quaint Redeemer's darkened facade
in the Giudecca canal and St. Mark's bay, in the black
waters of the ferryboat and Alilaguna, the ducal palace
level with the lapping water has seen it all before.*

The Square

Giulia, youben down
to the square yet?
Bar Fortuna!

Not yet. Benout
cleaning up the mess
from last night's storm.
You know our potted ginkgo?
Got knocked down again.
That north wind arrives
and blinco! down goes
the ginkgo.

You know Oscar
in the square?
A baby gang
broke in last night and
stole all the doughnuts
from the display
the papers say.

You gotta be kidding!
The bald-headed guy?
Those are the leftovers,
the ones he throws away.
People, what luck; you
just can't tell I say.

The Plague, July 7, 2022

Did you hear the latest?

Probably, what's up?

Fish fell from the sky in the streets
of San Francisco today; first they
washed ashore in Bolinas Lagoon
like a million shimmering beads.

Nothing surprises me now. I only ask,
Where's next? Who's next? When, why
and how? I'm a fan of Pinocchio's.

The scientists say it all makes sense:
Due to a marine heat wave the anchovies,
a boom or bust species, boomed. Then
a guild of ravenous whales cornered them
in the cloistered lagoon where they ran
out of water and life-giving oxygen.

Here in Venice and Lido we also have
a boom, a ceaseless surge of tourists
forcing residents to flee for breathing room
to mainland Mestre. And the falling fish?

The hustling roof-top gulls began
to hoist as many as beak could carry;
duelled wing to wing for booty
in the air, driving the losers to drop
their cache upon the city. They call it
kleptoparasitism, but people on the street
say, Look! today is Friday and it's raining
fish from the sky today. Oh Lordy!

Snowing in Casamazzagno

(November 22, 2019)

It's snowing over Casamazzagno this morning.
It catches in the tall grasses of the fields
but not on the road through town;
it tops the branches of the firs and fruit trees
and blankets the steep garden lots behind the houses
but not the road out of town;
it whitens the village roofs and the roof of
San Leonardo and the churchyard off the square
but not the highway below the town;
it builds in the corners of the piazza and
gathers along the gutters of the narrow streets,
but not on the doorsteps and entrance ways
where the old men and women are out sweeping.
The men in the town leave early in darkness
while the women come and go throughout the day:
they go to Padola, Santo Stefano, and Sesto;
they go to Belluno, Auronzo, and Brunico
for a visit to the hospital or health clinic,
to do the day's shopping at Passuello market,
to bring their teenage children to the bus stop
or train station in another town nearby or faraway.

The snow falls in sheets over the town cemetery,
shrouding the names on the headstones and tombs:
the cemetery, where the names cast cryptic shadows
over the town's daily diaspora, the names the living
find themselves in, the backward vision springing
from their small matter. The names recall those who
once lived and worked in the fields around the town
and did not have to go afar in order to stay.

Shell Game

Along the Lido's beaches in fall and winter
Giulia and Willi often take an hour's stroll,
starting from the abandoned Hotel des Bains
down past the hospital's ruins to San Nicolò,
if it's not too cold or damp or windy and the sun
is shining and the day is clear and they both
decide they're fit, and the sea is quiet enough
for them to confess the floating fragments
of last night's dream or scare helped along
by the rhythmic whispering outgoing tide;
but above all for Willi who loves to collect
different kinds and shapes of shells tossed up
by the outlandish chorus of waves in a sequence
of mini epiphanies, as if the lazy Adriatic
were playing a game with him alone, Willi.

Primed for the watery gambol
he spots one as it rolls
almost in reach,
a sudden flash of pink,
he stoops and stretches a hand
into the already receding wave;
missing once, he tilts
precariously forward
knowing he must be wary
(yet quick)
not to pull a muscle
while keeping his eye
on the striated scallop
(its dazzling fluted edges)
quickly tumbling away;
almost frantic now, he decides
to try a high-stakes leap

no matter how deep
the arrhythmic outgoing wave;
for even were he to agree
with Giulia that
there are many shells
just like it on the shore
a mere two steps away,
he knows at a glance
that each cast of the sea
is a personal summons
and every shell a prize,
for its odd combination
of color, shape and size.

Willi has long believed
it is the shells themselves
that beckon in a subtle undertow,
impossible to explain unless
you too are a collector and
credit each one of them
with being part of
an accretive design,
a collection, which
he keeps for the moment
in a casual heap
on his studio desk,
never caring to impose
an order that only the sea
may properly disclose.

Seeing this chaotic array
and pondering his aesthetic
dilemma, Giulia
decided to gift him
a small flat box
to put a choice selection

of his favorites within
a sort of picture frame
with the idea that he
could always rotate
and rearrange them
in order to contemplate
their infinite relations of
size, color, and shape from
day to day, as the muse
befits; especially if he
placed the box on the shelf
of the bathroom window
in front of where he sits
on his throne for somber
spells, as a ritual part
of his awakening hour.

Then one day as oft betides
in life's watery disarray
something unforeseen transpired
and Giulia alone was there
to wave the blame away:
in cleaning Willi's throne room
one day Marì in a hurry
took the clutter of shells
in Giulia's cast-off
cosmetic box on the dusty shelf
for things of meaningless value.
And so they disappeared,
just like that, without design
or bother; for in the end,
as Giulia tried to explain
on Marì's behalf, shells are
merely shells unless you
chance to glimpse one gleaming
in the lapping waves, rolling
towards you almost out of reach.

Growing up with Tornadoes

Summers growing up we village kids
rode tornadoes like ponies in our backyards
and I'm talking Wisconsin in the fifties.
Like a wild bull they scared our mother silly,
scattered us peewee leaguers in the park
home in a cloud of panic and glee,
tossed us about in a silent film blow-up
of wayward dogs and dairy debris.

The things we did at home became routine:
we handcuffed the curtains and lassoed
our bikes, scoped the yard for flying things,
tackled hysterical laundry as it ran away,
while Sparky, ruffled by menace of rain,
barked against his chain, outroared by
whoop of wind tearing at his mane.
We took him with us down the steps
of the fruit cellar beamed with spider webs,
closed the wooden doors and listened
hushed, for the huff and puff of Old Hurrah
pausing, then stomping past our beating heart.

These derelict memories from another country
and a distant past, where every village boy was
Huckleberry and every girl a Huckleberry too,
are worth their weight in scold and gospel true.
The last few years in the Lido lagoon, when
the July heat for us elders becomes extreme,
our barrier island suffers sudden downbursts
as the neighbor's lawn chairs jump the fence.

I know a tornado when I see one; just yesterday,
I glimpsed the gulls take off in a batlike flurry,

heard the snap of awnings whop-awhopping,
and I knew for sure we had one coming down.
Those ostinato clouds in the booming sky above
spelled *tornado* (twist the word however you will),
sending Giulia and me tripping in a pas de deux
to adapt my old routine to our sultry island milieu.

Convivium: At the Breakfast Table

Giulia, do you remember
the street and house number
where you once lived
when growing up, a kid?

No, why should I?
Why do you ask?

That's exactly why
you're always losing
your reading glasses
around the flat.
You forget we're
only guests on earth,
living off our credit cards.

Not everything is important
in the same way. For me
belonging is more meaningful
than insignificant facts
like a rusty house number.

Remember, the past was
once what today is.

No, today this very moment
everything is possible; growing up
not everything happened.

If you're always losing your
glasses how can anything ever
be clear? For me, we can explain
things. My childhood haunts are

choked with unbidden memories.

No matter, memory is not
about remembering, it's
about being aware of
what's possible today.

Circumstances come
first, *Giulia mia*, then
come compatibles,
feasibles and you.

Do you really think
an old address is
more than a rumor?
To Enrico Fermi
the sun's existence
was simply a storiella.

Calendrics

You know, Giulia,
memory has short wings.

Or no wings at all.

No, seriously,
you can't even agree
it's me who flipped
the calendar
to June today.

No, caro, it was me.
Just think a minute,
and be honest
with yourself
for once, okay?

Talking with you
is like trying
to spot a bird
that's already
flown away.

I know I flipped it
to June from May
because this month,
you may remember,
is my birthday.

There is no truth
in this house I see,
only personal interests,
sometimes base, and

ad personam arguments.

Your problem is you
have to learn to see
while you're looking
so that when you do
something significant like
changing the calendar,
you'll remember which
month we're talking about.
They may all seem
the same to you the way
the months fly by, no
reason to be ashamed.

No no. I know it's me
who changed the calendar
to June because last month's
bird was an *Acanthorhynchus*
tenuirostris. June's is a
Dacelo novaeguineae.

Very smart. You still think
Latin is better than Anglo-Saxon
when you want to make a point.
Anglo is for turning
the calendar; it's manual.
By the way, your state bird for
June is the Turdus migratorius,
just like you; mine here on the Lido
is the beautiful royal seagull.

Anyhow, I'm not arguing you are.
I know one thing, remembering
is the only place where you
can find yourself in. And you're

beginning to lose it; I know
it was me who remembered
to change the calendar to June.
I have a dentist's appointment
next week. Or why have
a calendar at all?

Okay, have it your way.
You changed the calendar
this morning and so did I.
One of us is telling the truth
the other a lie. What you remember
is a mental vision of another day
you changed the calendar, like seeing
a bird that has already flown away.

I will not tell her this morning
when she changed the calendar,
she flipped it to July instead of June,
probably confusing "Giulia" with
with *Luglio*, aiming to mark
the month and day of her
seventy-eighth birthday,
regardless of whether it's
the *Acanthorhynchus* or June's
Dacelo. Or even the *Turdus*
migratorius, that royal
migrating robin redbreast.

Giulia, *Imperfectio Caritatis*

Monday: pedicure for ingrown toenail, 9:00
Wednesday: mammogram at 11:30, Ospedale Civile
Friday morning: outdoor market, baguette and fruit,
       broccoli and fennel, *cicorietta* and *cipolline*
Friday afternoon: Johnson & Johnson Covid vaccine,
      Via Diego Valeri, 14:25
Saturday: fishmarket, *alici* or *polpo*; erboristeria: *Serenvit*a for Willi,
      Osteoflex for knee, *Bellavista* for Willi, *zinco* for energy
Sunday: Saverio e Giuliana, 17:00 *casa nostra*, *Lachryma Christi*
Monday: ferryboat strike, cancel car appointment

Anything else? ahyes: Willi's birthday tomorrow. Tiramisù?

Tiramisù Out of the World

In early morning light the kitchen
by force of will and pluck becomes
Giulia's calvary: a Disney gethsemane
sparkling from last night's dream; a site
for subverting Artusi's holy writ into
an antinomian tiramisù of arcane origin,
emerging from a delirium of cobbled
craft: irrational and messyanic, a fructification
of ingredients from the tinfoil covered
bowls of the refrigerator's bottom shelves,
the kitchen table an extrusion of half-
forgotten leavings and condiments.
                                        Catching Giulia
in actu is like peering into a convex mirror
of medieval theology or debauchery; her kitchen
a gnostic world turned upside down, a birthday
binge all for Willi, a feast of fools with tiramisù
served sacramentally after the evening news,
a sly rave with inner oohs and aahs, an ecstasy
of sugar a gush away from his own agnostic
coup de théâtre: "Tiramisù thou art and tiramisù
thou wilt remain," Willi mutters as he enters
Giulia's kitchen to turn it right side up again.

The Square

Hey there, Oscar,
how they hangin?
Boy that wind last night.
I heard you wanna
rent out Bar Fortuna. Is it
true? In case,
lemme know, okay?
I'll have a caffè macchiato caldo
and why not,
that cream cornetto there.
Be glad to get you
a fill-in.
The wife, you know.

I know what ya mean,
one job's not enough no more.
Takes two to put a loaf
on the table that's a fact.
I certainly will. No ifs
or buts. Then I can
chill out here like Willi
Minn and his wife,
watch the world from
a bench like local royalty.
The way things these days:
the square's become
a free-for-all. But not
just now, if things keep
rolling with all the German
tourists in town. I'll keep
you and the wifie in mind,
okay? No ifs or buts.

From Across the Atlantic

In the wee of
the morning of
this bell-lap year
I get a wake-up call
from brother Gari in Duluth
who booms me
back to our salad days
on grandpa's farm in
Stockbridge town
above Lake Winnebago,
with verses from our
favorite bard, who first
piped us down the rabbit
hole to poetry's wombroom.

Thinking about it
as the day darkens
here in via Lepanto
it dawns on me,
it took me all these seventy-
odd years of trans-
atlantic here and there
to become young.

These rising rungs
a ladder from the bar
of White Horse Tavern.

Once upon a time
I wouldn't have thought
twice about being easy
under the apple boughs.

Building Dwelling Dying

(elegy for an immigrant builder)

Years of effort
went

into planning and putting
up

this personal balance of
wall

and multiple geometries of
glass

so that the light will even
arrive

through the windowed planes of
roof

from a suddenly constant
outside

which comes tilting
in

at every angle of
day

and ever dawning
night

nearing from the woods
around

so that when the snow began
to build

and winter flickered in the tall
trees

and the heavens came down in
the clearing

you watched in your architect's chair
inside

not even inches
away

from pitching yourself
into

that zodiac drama of
moment

and the shadow play of
abiding form.

Susanna, Carry On!

PART I

First with those he most loved
                    and later alone
you scattered his ashes
                    in the places he minded,
where you often walked together:

you scattered them in the woods
                    surrounding the house
you scattered them over the water
                    along the peninsula shore
through the upper Michigan air;

you scattered him through
                    the pine-gated light
over leaf-layered root-weaved soil
                    of the rumpled decline
banking the creek down behind
                    the kitchen door;

like a sower you lavished,
                    over earth and water
through local green and blue
                    you portioned him
in the chosen places you knew
                    by heart, a neighborhood:
a weave of habit and memory.

PART II

With the ashes well-placed around you,
you sheered inward, lighter than ashes,
light as air, turning the world's weight
into the weird luster of letters gathered
from inside the house and the paths around.

You saved words from your walks, the dogs
ahead, to those places you haunted together
through the bosky neighborhood of ashes,
minding and remembering; during the clarion
hours of dawn and the fading lifelong day

you worked to cast the words in symbols
(soul-blown tares of eerie invasion);
then gleaned the symbols into lines,
lines as loose as raked up sticks from
the backyard pines but bundled by refrain.

You studied how to measure and compose;
there were many favorites (Emily, Robert,
Wendell, Nikki, Marianne and Elizabeth),
the charming locals too, met around a table at
caffeine seminars you could barely afford.

You mixed the written craft of others with
your own, at ease with *viva voce*. Now you
write daily, feeding a routine hunger; you
send me your favorite "poem a day" by
morning email and shyly add your latest.

Here and There

(A Letter from Susanna)

Walking out into
the grey, slightly
misting morning here
along Lido's internal canal,
sidling along the delivery
truck, engine thrum and
shoppers, whiff of
motor heat cappuccino
street café, *acqua alta*
at the lip of
Lepanto, a forelorn
peddler's folded
rainbow of scarves,
abruptly from behind
DingDing! a bicycle
brushing by:

and there you are,
alive and alone
holding out in your
upper Michigan woods,
a snowy paradise with snowy
walls which you build
shovel by shovel around you
as it snows and snows.
And suddenly you lose
your footing and falling,
jacknife backwards into
a hug of snow. And for
a floating moment you lay
absolutely still the wind,

the tall trees, vertigo
of pine and cloud
stirring far above,
sudden release upward
into your own snowy
frontyard cosmos.

I cannot help it,
walking, the mind of
me, confounds
and here you are.

A Poem for Gari

Abruptly in a fit of blue Giulia decides
to stir the alpine slumber of Willi's
psyche, asking, *Why have you never*
riffed about your younger brother so
dear to you, so close to your grieving?

Well, *cara*, it's rather late in the game
to be kicking up . . . truth is I own neither
the art nor brother Gari's dance of idioms
to capture his central self and seventy-year
perimeter – Gari, our family's poet laureate
and Duluth's too. I recall his Orphic muse
first frenzied him when he began to cull
poetic briefs of our riven family's thorn-
wrapped heart. Since our gruff immigrant
grandparents, their katzenjammer son
our dad and dear captive mother all died
in mill-town darkness, Gari vowed to write
wakes for them in elegiac portraits, aiming
to remind the world they too once hived.

In our no-care copfree days we first explored
metaphor's two-faced ways by snuggling
queerly at the bottom of our bathroom tub,
whispering *Breathe deep! Breath deep!* before
chanting the livid, bombastic protest poem
"Do Not Go Gentle into That Good Night" –
declaimed at father's funeral in a final farewell.
The bellowing lines of Thomas marked our
immersion in the roll of bardic voice which
my bro', gifted in song and meter, absorbed
to the bone. Our booming bathtub recitals
led me to Walt, Emily, and Sterling Brown, and

Gari to the cosmic wooshes of Whitehead
and Wise, a mad shot at taming the arcane
mysteries of metempsychosis before turning
the self-effacing details of family chronicle,
domestic chores like making bread or bending
over the ironing board, into figures of moment.

As a child Gari was a gay pudgy half-pint,
as gay as a June 8th sparrow, wagoning
down 125 South John in our nondescript
factory town along the polluted Fox.
Growing up we schooled together away
from home forever, huddled over the image
of a beloved community: huddling over
prayer at dawn and dusk, kneeling in the wild
woods of the Oneida tribal lands on Duck Creek;
bent over dense grammars taught by the same
robed masters (Latin, Greek, and French).
Pubescent novices, we puzzled extravagantly
over the dim contours of a phantom God,
during the canonical hours and the hushed
workouts of meditation; pulled back and forth
between the divine Plato's celestial theology
and the *materia prima* of Aristotle and Aquinas;
frequented the same terraced playing fields
and handball courts and walked the same
subdued corridors, learning to seek the day's
meaning in a casual remark, in dining hall
readings of lives of the saints, spells of *schola
cantorum*, study hall, and *silentium magnum*;
then twenty-minutes of scurrying before the dorm
lights went dark, launching sleep's brief amnesty
before the bells jarred us into a new day of
extraordinary routine, questing after the same
elusive ideal of a beloved community which
we, unsuspecting and boozy with earthly love,
were meant to embody.

You may be one in spirit, Willi, but you two hardly
inhabit one body. Gari lives what you only dream:
he puts his body on the line, beholds it in his verse.

Yes, my dear, but with one foot in the urn I
 have favored memory's myth of our brotherly
years together, boarding school years, when
our vague motherless souls, fresh from the family
warzone, stood gleeing between heaven and hell
as we learned to gird ourselves like Paul, Gandhi,
Dorothy Day, Solanus Casey and saintly Minnie
with the heroic virtues and a higher law beaming
beyond social compliance and village bickering.
All the rest, the daily routine? Mere application.
Mired in the fumes of Carson's toxic spring
but marrowed with metaphor's transports, Gari
explores through verse a limpid gospel code,
sole heir to mother's silver unschooled heart:
it takes two to make love, two to think beyond
the self, two to become human, two to be free,
and the image of a beloved community to trans-
form our fallen world, our lost humanity.

Paradox

Giulia, do you remember
these two maxims of
Martin Luther's? They help
to center our status
as surplus beings
here in via Lepanto:

"A Christian is a perfectly
free lord of all, subject
to none."

"A Christian is a perfectly
dutiful servant of all,
subject to all."

Sounds like Saint Paul or
Augustine's two cities;
a wily way of glossing
the calendar leap from
Sunday to Monday; or
what of the gothic bond
between the German
princes and their serfs,
minus the Sunday magic.
Then there's us early
risers, lords in the morning
and beggars before
that evening sun goes down.

The Bible alone, not that pile
of stone, Saint Peter's, was
our *fratellino's* rock
with nothing but a whim

between the plowman
and the Word.

Lordship for Luther
comes with the freeing
power of faith, then
comes justification
and the Christian's claim
to spiritual sovereignty.
A matter of whim, Giulia:
a sky hook for us fading
baby boomers, our shelf
life about to expire in
this housebound outpost
above the beckoning plastic
glitter of the canal below.

Sovereignty yes, but in heaven
not here in the Lido, right?
I'm not howling for help
from the Salvation Army,
but lording it over
this rebellious body
keeps me busy all seven.

Here in via Lepanto Luther
counsels simple obedience
to the local police, our governors
high and low – even if
another Führer comes along.

Not so fast, Willi the clerk!
Trouble broke out when
Müntzer and Müller began
reading Daniel in Luther's Bible:
scripture-shoed peasant bands

rallied around the redeeming Word,
Capital and Labor in a deadly
Siamese dance. Oh Katherina,
boss of Zuhlsdorf and obedient
wife, it's time to take our nap,
Oh Lordy.

Luther Goes Shopping at the COOP

We've come a long way since Luther's day,
when the red hot potato was religion not
the market. Now it's the Bitcoin, even
if the claims of Martin and his caravan of
saints still echo in our COOP's current ad:
The COOP Is You! And that rival foodstore:
People Over Things! Talk about secularization.

You mean sexualization. Lusty Martin made
the COOP possible, don't you see? Religion
didn't disappear, it just cross-dressed.

*   *   *

Talk about lordship, My God! You enter
this air-conditioned heaven in overheated
August – with everyone and everything,
truly all of creation at your beck and call,
and you find there's so much to believe in!

And it's easy to binge in here. A world
lit up so bright, like seeing for the first
time! No trouble finding the items on my
list; although I need my reading glasses
to detect how much sugar they've added
to the bread in order to sweeten the salt.

Beyond imagination, Giulia! Beyond grief.
Today's Friday special, Zwingli sausages flown
in from Zurich; tender chicken breasts ideal
for Erasmus's delicate stomach; shelves of pills
and laxatives for Martin's blocked up bowels.

You go up and down these aisles feeling
you were part of a glorious procession of
saints, with no leader or laggard, first or last,
a continuous gyre of shoppers devotedly
studying the deals. We're all royalty at check out:
"Hi, honey, how ya doin'? Can I bag that
for you?" Almost otherworldly! I feel like I'm
a queen in here, just like at the hairdresser's.

But then it ends and we have to go back outside
with all our bags, back into the real world.

What real world you mean? The one we just left,
that heaven on earth, or the one with our rusty
bicycles and your flat tire? You tell me. And there
by the door stands Destiny, that new Nigerian
migrant, doing a brisk business gleaning shoppers'
loose change and bully to help old ladies with
their bags. You can bet he thinks Italy is one big
COOP with that purring automatic door opening
and closing: What's that saying? Things over People!

Uh-huh, I see it now, a matter of cash or crashing
in: the sweat-free COOP, my wallet's flat tire, and
a biblical flow of climate migrants at the door.

Jeffrey's Beat

Jeffrey, one of
      three Nigerians
            who commute daily

from Mira to the Lido
      by bus and boat
            come rain or shine

and stand forever
      outside the Lido's
            three COOP supermarkets,

wedged between
      the shopping carts,
            wastebins and bicycles,

takes in around
      ten to fifteen Euros
            on a tiptop summer morning

before making the rounds of
      the boulevard's soft spots:
            the shops, caffès, and kiosks,

rarely exchanging
         a personal word or
            two with a local

who knows his name,
      knows he's Yoruba or even,
            "Hey man, how's the game?"

Here along via Lepanto I spy him
        rolling towards me,
                bouncing left and right

a pinball among
        the shoppers, tourists
                and wheelchair pensioners,

right arm shooting out
        palm open seeking
                coin in the eye, contact,

pressing a grooved
        hard-luck story about
                his bad knee or sore stomach;

or like April last,
        about his mother's coming
                birthday in May a month away,

she alone now, in her late
        seventies, bedridden,
                and not doing well and

how he was saving up
        for a plane ticket to Lagos,
                600 Euros will do it:

"Could you help me, *mi
        aiuti*? I have to make it home,
                only 50 Euros, Mr Willi, pleeeze.

I must see Mama
        one last time,
                she's old, not well, alone!"

Thirty days later,
       Jeffrey is still at his
              station by the COOP

still bumming for
       that magic sum,
              the gleanings always good

for the daily commute
       from Mira to Lido and back,
              the rest didn't matter anymore.

Insomnia

You know what?

Yes, I do.

Life's absurd.

If you think it so.

Life's a turd.

If you make it so.

The world is poisoned.

Is that a metaphor?

I'm a stranger to myself.

Don't be nostalgic!

It's slipping through my. . .

You mean your toes?

It's my body not my mind.

At seventy odd it may be both.

It's a philosophical problem,
isn't it?

*You're foundering in poetry,
aren't you?*

Buona notte . . . *Uh-huh.*

Bar Fortuna

People are crazy, the counter man
at Bar Fortuna mused. One morning
all the cornetti are gone by nine.
The next, five are still on the tray
at noon and gotta be thrown away.
People! . . . you just can't tell, I say.

Einklammerung

(October 9, 2023)

Willi, Willi, my charming
old one, why so mooding?
It's too late in the day
to cheer you on but
for thingamajig's sake,
Cheer up! I see your
blood is up, is it their
nihilism and jihad *bêtise*?

These killings, my dear,
These killings. They're beasts:
children, seniors, that woman
in a wheel chair. What's
a human life anymore?
Everybody's nobody there.
In the pan-eye of the socials
we're all hostages for now.

And that open air prison
with 2.3 million people
walled in and locked up?
No state, no rights, but
a people all the same.
Their whatchamacallit
wardens: beasts by another
name and other rules. But
beasts all the same.
From gate to gate, one big
target: buildings, trees,
one big . . . refugees.
Top Varmint Gallant orders

the strip's "complete closure":
"No electricity, no food, no
water, no fuel." No Life?

We ourselves are nothing.
Our word is nothing. What
we stand for nothing.
From this day forward I refuse
the confines of all identity
groups: we're what's left
without them, if only we could
wiggle free: race, age, nationality,
sex, gender, class, color, what else?
All prompts for a funeral oration.

You missed a major trap, stand-
point, like us here in via Lepanto:
geography, as in Palestinian. A view
from a point, spume of life ablaze.

Just Talking

Willi, let's talk a minute. Ever since
we've backed into being senior citizens –
oh how long ago? – all your ritual fuss
about feeling on top of the world since
being retired (stubby dodos, big-beaked
and soon to be extinct) and the editor
of our local leftist rag likes the selfie
for your obit, doesn't faze me a whit.

Top or bottom, how I feel doesn't matter
a fig about our status as human capital.
Being fully human remains an open door,
for you an otherworldly grail. Otherwise
how could we wake up at five and not feel
utterly grim? We're pinched between two
despotic limits: birth and death, cheers
and tears. What happens in between? Bare
chronicle at best, meaningless without
a beginning or an end.

Dio mio, Willi, I thought by now you'd want
to abandon your sacerdotal rant for a scat
of reality! All metaphysics, no common sense.
Who still believes in the claim we're all
born equal, me a queen and you whatever?
Sovereignty doesn't factor anymore. We're
old, merely the sum of our aches and pills,
a biological abstraction like Marx's worker.
You really want to feel your worth? Swear
in the square! Carry a sign! Or jump over
the broom with me behind the Big House.
You know what I mean, I know you know.

Uh-huh. An act you say, not an inner resource
or right to recognition apart from where we live
and who we know. But here's the rub, where
do you think our acts originate? We're not human
because of the way we act, but because we are.
Hitler was a monster because he was human
and didn't act like it. You for example: it's your
bad knees and 41 kilos that explain the way
you act, not who you are, here in via Lepanto.
We made a vow to live together fifty years ago
and here we sit, with all our hurt humanity.

Maybe I should make a pan of tiramisù, huh?
A funeral cake for friends who'll want to attend
your wake. I'll check if I need to hit the COOP
for ingredients. Oh, one more thing. Your notion
of us wingless angels sounds like Ronnie's joke
of 1971: "If you've seen one tree, you've
seen them all." But what if it's an oak in late
autumn and not an evergreen? That'd make
a difference when sitting by the window, huh?
I'll go check for ladyfingers. I want to add
a little fake news to a recipe I found in Artusi.

Wait, Giulia! When I went for the paper this morning
Bar Fortuna had a display of tiramisù in little cups
that looked divine, the day's specialty; my buddy
Oscar said Hurry, they'll be gone by noon. About
angels, what's the connection with Ronnie's shrubs?

You mean trees? If all of us humans belong to
a single genus, then there's really no need to chat
with neighbors in via Lepanto, since your abstract
humanity swallows up all our quirks. For me,
what makes us human is sharing a common space
together, sitting around a table in the square,

plotting how to plant a row of trees by night
along the canal; give the Lido a leafy face instead
of cutting them down for parking space. Get it?

What kind of trees you going to plant in place of
the cars? As many as there are stumps? That would
jazz things up. Oh, when googling for tropicals,
you better start with "Tree." Know what I mean?

The Other Side

(Willi and Giulia, transatlantic)

If only I had stayed on the banks of the old Midwest:
a student of Saukenuk, Rock Island, and the big river,
talking up the wolf, Black Hawk, and Blue Mound,
instead of tailing the *barone* with briefcase in tow
from one conference bluff to another – a fog-eyed
year torquing his rambling mss and bowwow prose
into token Americanese: *Ich könnte nicht anders.*

The grass is always greener on the other side
of customs! Digging up the past with "what if".
You'll never know Willi till the day you die how
lucky you were to teach Old English in Trieste
in the shadow of Joyce, bingeing on my gourmet
bag lunches, my rearview existentialist. Time
to forget and say goodbye for æfre to ill will!

Reasoning with Willi is pointless. The Lido appears
lost to him, his childhood home a sunflower, tertium
non datur! *Progression, pattern, a meaningful life:*
all are due to memory's backward glance and spots
of time culled from that other Atlantic shore. Then came
flight and his love-sick crash on this fishlike isle, whose
liquid air sealed Willi the student in amber, fixed him
here among the city's stolen marbles, yet never wholly
here: Hier stehe ich, So wahr mir Gott helfe.

Ciao!

I saw you on Delta flight DL193
at 3,590 feet among the clouds
in mid-ocean on my way
from VCE to NYC. You came
out of the toilette into
the semi-dark corridor
your hair slicked back
and dressed to kill (a whiff
of Old Spice you once dabbed
behind my ears) as if
it was a Saturday evening
and you were off to Primo's
for a few brews with buddies
while Mom at home stayed bent
over her weekend ironing board.
You walked quickly, looking
straight ahead, like an apparition,
and I didn't even get a chance
to call out or say *Hello*
I was so surprised.

Sovereignty, Loss of the World

PART I

Dear *Pittima*, since we've retired I feel
it's no longer our world anymore. Where
has it gone? We spend our time looking
out the window, floating above the Lido
as if we were in outer space, cut free.

Outer space, you'd never pass the physical.
You need to have talent, pull, and SpaceX
to orbit the Earth these days. Now that we
know of all those other galaxies, looking out
and up makes feeling weightless heavenly.
Earth's an old shoe with a hole in its soul.

Well, I'm talking action, making a mark
in this world, moving among peers, planning
a trip. Why don't we study maps anymore?
Staring at other planets is for an idle Sunday
with snotty tots at the Lido's planetarium.

Well, Willi, you're just pining and whining
the same as forty years ago. That's just you.
And what's wrong with the company of children?
You didn't plan anything back then either.
You came to Venice on a dime, a gamble:
with Lukacs, a photo of me in your pocket,
and a thesis on Goldmann to write. You came
for me, remember?

I don't know. That was fifty years ago.
Certainly I came for you. But there was an urgent
sense of reckoning everywhere, the air crackling

with student revolt. Things were about to explode.
Strikes, sit-ins. We were angry, unconsolable, and
underneath it all there was you and me. Yes, it was
you and just us two.

Yes, on top of it all there was us;
tied together by your Yankee doodling. Me with one
foot on the ground teaching Italglish, you with two
in the air and a scholarship to keep you here.
We clung to each other a day at a time, remember?

Clinging? We clung to ideas and life on the streets,
scrawling manifestos against the State. With hearts
calmly wild we hugged against the war outside.
Remember? Of course, who cared about memory
when our blazing imaginations were busy charting
revolution in front of Ca' Foscari's chained gates.

PART II

We were only floating, just like now, looking
for a place to survive, a way to stay together,
here or across the Atlantic, far away in the USA.
I confess, I had no mind to leave Venice for a life
in some sleepy college town with its plantation
campus, towering stadium and guzzling fraternities.

You think I wasn't beguiled by the delirious song
of European *franc-tireurs*? Look at these stacks
and shelves of books. We read in a fever: Lukacs,
Gramsci, Althusser; Jakobson, Barthes and Eco;
Benjamin, Horkheimer, Habermas, and Adorno.

Hannah Arendt, Maria Corti and Julia Kristeva;
Luce Irigaray, Hélène Cixous and Agnes Heller;

Gayatri Spivak, Sylvia Wynter, and Edna Brodber.
Oh, and Simone de Beauvoir and Germaine Greer!

What about Hall and Gilroy at Birmingham?
Césaire, Senghor, Fanon and Eric Williams;
Lyotard, Derrida, Deleuze, and Foucault!

Tel Quel, *the* New Left Review, *and* Rinascita*;*
Berlinguer and the Italian Communist Party!
Everything furtively linked to the vendors' cries
at Rialto market, the cicchetti *dives and demijohns.*

Ca' Foscari was our gathering place to read, dispute,
and build a résumé; form leftist cadres and student
cohorts against the ruse of capitalist happiness, the end
of history, and the tourist buyout of our sinking
city, a money machine for trifling fashion merchants.

We thrived in seminars and preached with bullhorns.
The future was now and ours to forsake, but it didn't
seem that way. Today a five-year-old was riding her
tricycle in St. Mark's Square when a vigile *warned her,*
Don't disturb the tourists walking here. What did we
teach, what accomplish? How did the city lose its way?

Dark Sovereignty, Decreation

You know, Willi, I could live happily in a world
the size of a walnut and consider myself its queen
if I didn't have to hear you fluorescing about our
loss of world and flickering humanity. Can't we
learn to be content with what we have and are,
with or without our sovereignty? (Sad Willi is
deaf to common sense and my advice; his gloom
begins to glow, Oh Lordy!)

Sovereignty's dark side in old age begins
with the pensioner's dole, then come
the declining powers of memory, eyes and arm,
the need of an afternoon nap countered by
insomnia and a mood of regret: the enclitics of age
governed by a shelf of drugs, unnamed waves
of pain, the penury of bodily vigor, incontinence,
wild eyebrows, loss of hearing and appetite.
And what about our diminishing circle of friends?
The metronome of their departure marks our days.
Once its circumference spanned the Atlantic; now
our Lido amity lines are slack, as homeless
friendship wanders lost along Lepanto canal.

Weary Willi! Stop your groveling, lift up your
heavy heart. More Erasmus and less Augustine!
Let the bedroom's early light light up your mind;
renounce the doctrine of despair if only for me.
Even the Lido's seniors gracing the public square
are happy in their wheelchairs and assisted living,
a whispering caste hallowed by their helplessness
and ancient ways. Look to the poet's words, she
serves best who sits in silence waiting out her days.

Willi's Will

Giulia, what about my books?
Nobody wants them here.
What'll you do with them
when I'm gone? Promise me.

What do you want, you leave
your name and a nest egg
in the States. You better start
writing a will. You may not
be able to hand down all
those books but you can leave
a lengthy inventory.

My brother's children they
don't even know me, I
won't even haunt them
once I've crossed the bar.
They don't read books.
They have no love for
me or forlorn Italy, only
for the local scene in
Calumet and Eden, where
they live and do not lack.

Giulia shakes her head
and says nothing. Then
she notes, The family
name is an omen. It weighs
like a burden on those
who bear it. It's on their
report cards and diplomas,
above all in their bones.
You're part of the tree,
more root than branch.

Maybe these poems
about life along the canal
in via Lepanto, the pleasures
of being-in-excess on the benches
of the Lido's public square,
will catch their curiosity,
stir them to chart a genealogy
when their children demand,
Are there any plums on our
wild crabapple tree?

Giulia shakes her head
and says nothing. Then she
notes, They'll find the dates,
the places, and our names
and use their imaginations
to sketch us back into life,
although that life will be
mostly of their making.

Yes, of course, how
could it be otherwise?
I better get back to work
on the poems, patent them
so memory will confine their
midwestern imaginations.

Giulia, who has an older brother
but no kin, neither nephews
nor godchildren, nobody near
or far to remember her, shakes
her head and says nothing.

Endbed, Nostos

Early morning radio,
the queen working
the dial in the dark:

tango
harbor hall
no foot tax
just us two

TAP AND SWING
MOVE IN MEASURE
SLIDE AND BEND

before phlebo
and late morning
morphine

Care Home

(Et in arcadia Willi)

In the morning the bed:
stripped and exposed
to sea air and seagull
behind the fluttering curtains.

The nurses, ruddy and quick,
prop me up with a biblical quip,
sleeve and comb me to a slick
as if I were going on a trip.

From the hall comes noon and the new
sheets snapped wide like sails,
their billowing locked down tight
at the four corners of the circled bed
in the whirring air of the vaulted room.

Soup and sandwich served on a tray
a sleepless nap, a game of solitaire;
then the doctor's glare holds sway,
"Now lay him down with care."

Inevitable evening ascends and sleep
to make amends, cool folds of night
over the floating bed descend.
Delivered in ghostly gown onto this bark,
ferryboat with the crackling sails,
I shroud myself bend knees to chin
embrace the gauzy chill until
heart's faint heat rises from within.

Ready now, *cast off.* Now's the time
of ascendance, a finality
of immanence. Lord, I will not
pray to stay another day.

Eyes Wide Open

Poor daft Willi the wolf
from dawn till dusk till
the very last day descanted
the abstract value of human
life tempered by Puccini
arias and the jump blues
of early Louie Prima amidst
the death of peace in Palestine
(the) Ukraine Sudan Syria
Myanmar Yemen Afghanistan
Chad Benin Democratic Republic
Of Congo Iraq South Sudan
Columbia Cameroon Uganda
Ghana Ivory Coast Libya
Mexico Mali Mozambique
Mauritania Niger Somalia
Nigeria Togo Tanzania
Russia Burkina Faso Ethiopia
weekly migrant drownings
in the dream-soaked waters
of Pontus son of Gaia and
the end of nature, panting
in his very last breath: *Ca ci*
su lupi e forsi vui sapiti
Si ci su lupi vui ne canusciti
Ci boni su li paroli di li muti.

King Willi Passing

(Queen Giulia attends)

The king has gone
to his eternal rest.
All his senses gone
it's surely for the best.

I waited near the ghostline
       at hand's edge
              in the sheeted room,
until your breath let go
       in a hoarse *hrumpff*
              like a fugitive balloon.

A supple radiance
       of spirit spent,
              you became dead weight.
And I? no longer a lady waiting,
       I pass through hospice walls
              back into life, never too late.

Home along Lungomare's half-dawn
       I open to a shuffling
              beyond the study door;
Then, as if a voice, hapheard –
       Pippín! Pippín! the papers whirred
              in a dervish dance on the study floor.

Sei tu? Son qua. So mi. Before
       moving to close the window
              against the king's supreme chicanery.

Giulia Writes an Elegy

From the very beginning
wherever Willi wandered,
whether down in the village
or to some other town, like Costa
or Danta in the upper mountain valley,
he found himself looking
for the ocre-colored belltower
of San Leonardo, the little sculpted
chapel completed in 1545
by *magister* Ruopel *murator teutonicus*,
perched like a watchman
above the zigzag streets
of Casamazzagno: a beacon,
or maybe enchanting mushroom
for all the town to see and silently claim,
but which few now cared to consider.
Or is it an ancient telecom tower,
as Willi joked it was, for those
who disdain Twitter and Telegram
and are waiting for some life-saving
message only it can provide,
one already coded in the ringing
of the hours both early and late,
the tolling of the hours
both early and late?

Giulia, the *Accabadora*

A few months after scattering Willi
along the western shores of Lake
Winnebago and living now neither
in heaven nor on earth, Giulia, a fairy
thirty-eight kilos of surplus memory,
shapes the remains of her local
mobility into Sunday morning visits
to the Lido's planetarium, lining up
with the island's tots (her *figlie
d'anima*) or in calm study of the stars
evenings on the balcony next to
Willi's potted envoy, the ginkgo.

Then late one autumn evening
with royal fanfare, when a cloudless
sky lit up the canal with liquid stars,
Giulia, Lido's legendary *pittima*,
disappeared in a flash, with only
a neighbor to witness her passage.

Willi was right in the end, nobody
wanted his annotated books whatever
the subject or century, neither
the Hugo Pratt library nor his former
Ca' Foscari colleagues. For a new
paradigm now raged, the age imposed
the infosphere: ebooks, Internet,
Big Data, and AI. With the persistence
of a mouse, Giulia tallied Willi's
books and cruised the dying antiquaries
far and near, to no avail. The books
lay orphaned in the flat for years,
Giulia their spectral custodian and

sole visitant. The whirring she half-
heard in Willi's study the morning
he died was due to a hidden fracture
in the floor long buried to the ceiling
under stalagmite stacks of scrapped
political philosophy from Plato and
More to Marx, Gramsci and Schmitt.

Growing deafer as time passed
and caring only to map the farthest
planets on her wall-sized sky chart,
Giulia paid no heed to the creeping
fissures spreading from the study floor
like a living claw, until it was too late.

One night the blazing trail of a falling
star lit up the balcony like a movie set,
the transcendent light concealing a core
of immanence in the form of Willi.
Had her Houdini come back for her?
Willi, sei tu? son qua, Giulia blurted into
the quaking flare. *So in the end it's me
and you, just us two?* He seemed to
beckon, quivering mightily to deliver
a particle of sound, *What?* into the starry
night. Seeing the core of light fade
as quickly as it came she whispered
quietly to herself in reply, *Nothing*.

Only with Willi's astral return did Giulia
come alive to the quaking vibrations she
had felt underfoot for months: The books
in Willi's study! They're moving in rows,
an army! When in a flicker the blazing
form lifted, it left a blinding wake
of blackness and an empty balcony.

According to a hazy video Giulia's
neighbor posted on Facebook the day
after, here is what happened: While
the church bells tolled midnight,
a freakish flash of light lit up the palace
in via Lepanto as it came buckling down
in a thunderous bang, collapsing inward,
down into the canal below. And Giulia?
Robed in her white astronomer's gown,
her arms outspread like wings, she appeared
at once to lift off among the fleeing gulls
and plunge downwards into the canal,
surrounded by thousands of volumes,
their open pages fussing like an entourage
as Giulia disappeared in the waters below.

Notes to the poems

SOVEREIGNTY: With the American and French Revolutions, royal sovereignty was magically invested in the people, who became the holders of inalienable rights. These rights – such as the right to life, liberty, and the pursuit of happiness – were no longer bestowed but were considered inborn and universal, although initially not for people of African descent. In the twenty-first century, the age of mass migrations, global conflicts, and multicultural democracies, these rights, further elaborated in 1948, have remained largely abstract and often without meaning. They need to be politically reclaimed and made concrete. Among the weakest segments of the population, elderly people, once considered an integral and important part of family and community life, are largely relegated to the status of beings-in-excess. Their condition of irrelevance is emblematic of the deeply negative drift of capitalist societies, particularly in the rich, fortress-like nations of the Global North.

"*Endgame,*" gloss: "And to make an end is to make a beginning. The end is where we start from."

T. S. Eliot, "East Coker," *Four Quartets*

"*Dear Moon, July 2020*" gloss: "Biography is the mesh through which our real life escapes." Tom Stoppard

"*Spheres of Influence,*" gloss: "I may not understand what you're saying but I know what you mean." A popular saying.

"*Giulia, Reading Virgil in Bed,*" gloss: her epic adventure, "where everything is make-believe but nothing false."

"*A Kingdom of Prospects,*" gloss: Remembering King Philip of Macedon's tomb at Vergina, Greece.

"*Growing Farther and Farther Together*," gloss: The *caffettiera* is a little two-cup espresso affair.

"*Willi to his Muse*," gloss: a wink at Encolpius's confessional prayer to Priapus in Petronius's *Satyricon*.

"*Backyard Cosmology*," gloss: Giulia's afterthought: "now that I think of it."

"*The Two Bodies of the Queen*," subtitle from T.S. Eliot, "The Waste Land" (first draft), with a wink at Ernst Kantorowicz's *The King's Two Bodies*.

"*Sovereignty, What?*" Pittima: The *pittima*'s public role in the Venetian Republic was to follow a debtor and cry out their debt so as to embarrass them and get them to pay up. The *pittima*, a woman dressed in red so that people would better be able to spot the debtor, was chosen from the lower classes and received social assistance and lodging for her efforts. Later, the word became synonymous with a woman who is always complaining.

"*Cousin Nori, Where Are We Now?*" gloss: "Like ancient trees, we die from the top." Gore Vidal, *Julian*.

"*Wild Weather, Lido di Venezia*," gloss: The wind coming from Trieste is called "the Bora," a little hurricane.

"*Shell Game*," gloss: "It is invariably oneself that one collects." Jean Baudrillard, "The System of Collecting."

"Convivium: *At the Breakfast Table*," gloss: "Where two people agree one is surely superfluous." Yiddish saying.

"*Giulia*, Imperfectio Caritatis," gloss: "Although there may be a hierarchy apparent in the list, additional items can always be added to the written list itself." Robert E. Belknap, *The List*.

"*From Across the Atlantic*," gloss: "Only they who live, not in time but in the present, are happy." Wittgenstein, *Notebooks, 1914 – 1916*.

"*Einklammerung*," gloss: Edmund Husserl's term for bracketing or phenomenological reduction. By bracketing perception, one suspends judgment about the world of everyday, burdened with its cultural scripts and biases, in order to analyze one's experience of it.

"*The Other Side*," gloss: Echoing Luther, "I couldn't do otherwise" and "Here I stand. So help me God."

"*Sovereignty, Loss of the World*," Part II, gloss: As of August 2022, Venice's population dipped under 50,000. In the 1950s the city numbered over 150,000. On August 14, 2022, over 80,000 tourists invaded the city. (*La nuova di Venezia*)

"*Willi's Will*," gloss: "All goes onward and outwards, nothing collapses / And to die is different from what anyone supposed, and luckier." Walt Whitman, from stanza 6, "Song of Myself."

"*Endbed, Nostos*," gloss: "Reality is the beginning not the end," Wallace Stevens, "An Ordinary Evening in New Haven."

"*Eyes Wide Open*," the song lyrics in English read: There are wolves around here, you might just know / Yes, there are, and we both know who they are / How beautiful are the words of the mute. (from the song "U lupu d'Asprumunti"). On the page facing this poem, Minn had copied out these lines from Georg Trakl's poem "On the Eastern Front": "A spiky no-man's-land encloses the town. / The moon hunts petrified women / from their blood-spattered doorsteps. / Grey wolves have forced the gates."

"*King Willi Passing*," gloss: "Who but the dead know what it is to be alive?" Morton Feldman, "Frank O'Hara: Lost Times and Future Hopes," *Give My Regards to Eighth Street: Collected* Writings. The Italian in the last stanza translates, "*Is it you? I'm here. It's me* (this last in Venetian)."

"*Giulia, the* Accabadora," gloss: An *accabadora* in Sardinian is a finisher, one who helps people die.

Acknowledgments

Quoted passages in "Squawk, A Genealogy" are from William Strachey, *A True Reportory* (http://virtualjamestown.org); Walt Whitman, "Crossing Brooklyn Ferry"; Henry James, *The American Scene*; Hart Crane, "To Brooklyn Bridge"

Wallace Stevens Journal: "Building Dwelling Dying"

La Stua (annual journal published for the town of Casamazzagno): "Giulia Writes an Elegy"

I wish to thank the following people for reading the sequence and offering their comments: Franca Bernabei, Caterina Edwards, Dennis Barone, Jacopo Aldrighetti, Gary Boelhower, Marco Loverso, Susan Griffith, John W. Lowe, the editors of Bordighera Press, especially Nicholas Grosso (sharp-eyed, astute, tolerant).

About the Author

WILLI Q MINN (1946-2020) died unattended in a hospital during the Covid epidemic. For decades he worked in the U.S., France, and Italy as a translator from French and Italian into English and apparently wrote poetry most of his life; but left almost all of it unpublished. After the clamorous collapse of the building at the corner of Lepanto and Marcantonio Bragadin, Lido di Venezia, where the Minns lived, boxes of notebooks filled with poetry were found cast into and across the Lepanto canal. The scholar William Boelhower, who lived nearby and had struck up an acquaintance with Giulia Minn, found several of these boxes near the garbage bins in via Lepanto and saved them from oblivion. In one of the notebooks, Minn had written a poetic sequence, a sort of Life Studies, dealing mostly with the closing years of two people who had traveled back and forth across the Atlantic all their lives and were now coping with the malaise of old age and society's expedient neglect, subtrahend for excessive government debt. Boelhower has edited the sequence without touching the poems themselves or their order of appearance. Many of the poems are accompanied by an illuminating gloss and translation where need be; these are provided in the Notes section at the end of the volume.

Editor's contact email: William.Boelhower@unive.it

VIA Folios

A refereed book series dedicated to the culture of Italians and Italian Americans.

DANIELA GIOSEFFI. *Blood Autumn/Autunno di sangue*. Vol 39. Poetry.

FRED MISURELLA. *Lies to Live By*. Vol 38. Stories.

STEVEN BELLUSCIO. *Constructing a Bibliography*. Vol 37. Italian Americana.

ANTHONY JULIAN TAMBURRI, Ed. *Italian Cultural Studies 2002*.
Vol 36. Essays.

BEA TUSIANI. *con amore*. Vol 35. Memoir.

FLAVIA BRIZIO-SKOV, Ed. *Reconstructing Societies in the Aftermath of War*.
Vol 34. History.

TAMBURRI. et al., Eds. *Italian Cultural Studies 2001*. Vol 33. Essays.

ELIZABETH G. MESSINA, Ed. *In Our Own Voices*.
Vol 32. Italian/American Studies.

STANISLAO G. PUGLIESE. *Desperate Inscriptions*. Vol 31. History.

HOSTERT & TAMBURRI, Eds. *Screening Ethnicity*.
Vol 30. Italian/American Culture.

G. PARATI & B. LAWTON, Eds. *Italian Cultural Studies*. Vol 29. Essays.

HELEN BAROLINI. *More Italian Hours*. Vol 28. Fiction.

FRANCO NASI, Ed. *Intorno alla Via Emilia*. Vol 27. Culture.

ARTHUR L. CLEMENTS. *The Book of Madness & Love*. Vol 26. Poetry.

JOHN CASEY, et al. *Imagining Humanity*. Vol 25. Interdisciplinary Studies.

ROBERT LIMA. *Sardinia/Sardegna*. Vol 24. Poetry.

DANIELA GIOSEFFI. *Going On*. Vol 23. Poetry.

ROSS TALARICO. *The Journey Home*. Vol 22. Poetry.

EMANUEL DI PASQUALE. *The Silver Lake Love Poems*. Vol 21. Poetry.

JOSEPH TUSIANI. *Ethnicity*. Vol 20. Poetry.

JENNIFER LAGIER. *Second Class Citizen*. Vol 19. Poetry.

FELIX STEFANILE. *The Country of Absence*. Vol 18. Poetry.

PHILIP CANNISTRARO. *Blackshirts*. Vol 17. History.

LUIGI RUSTICHELLI, Ed. *Seminario sul racconto*. Vol 16. Narrative.

LEWIS TURCO. *Shaking the Family Tree*. Vol 15. Memoirs.

LUIGI RUSTICHELLI, Ed. *Seminario sulla drammaturgia*.
Vol 14. Theater/Essays.

FRED GARDAPHÈ. *Moustache Pete is Dead! Long Live Moustache Pete!*.
Vol 13. Oral Literature.

JONE GAILLARD CORSI. *Il libretto d'autore. 1860 - 1930*. Vol 12. Criticism.

HELEN BAROLINI. *Chiaroscuro: Essays of Identity*. Vol 11. Essays.

PICARAZZI & FEINSTEIN, Eds. *An African Harlequin in Milan*.
Vol 10. Theater/Essays.

JOSEPH RICAPITO. *Florentine Streets & Other Poems*. Vol 9. Poetry.

FRED MISURELLA. *Short Time*. Vol 8. Novella.

NED CONDINI. *Quartettsatz*. Vol 7. Poetry.

ANTHONY JULIAN TAMBURRI, Ed. *Fuori: Essays by Italian/American
Lesbiansand Gays*. Vol 6. Essays.

ANTONIO GRAMSCI. P. Verdicchio. Trans. & Intro. *The Southern Question*.
Vol 5. Social Criticism.

DANIELA GIOSEFFI. *Word Wounds & Water Flowers*. Vol 4. Poetry. $8

WILEY FEINSTEIN. *Humility's Deceit: Calvino Reading Ariosto Reading Calvino.*
Vol 3. Criticism.
PAOLO A. GIORDANO, Ed. *Joseph Tusiani: Poet. Translator. Humanist.*
Vol 2. Criticism.
ROBERT VISCUSI. *Oration Upon the Most Recent Death of Christopher Columbus.*
Vol 1. Poetry.

www.ingramcontent.com/pod-product-compliance
Lightning Source LLC
Chambersburg PA
CBHW020207090426
42734CB00008B/969